Other books by G. Kim Blank

*Wordsworth's Influence on Shelley: A Study of
Poetic Authority*
The New Shelley: Later Twentieth-Century Views (ed.)
Influence and Resistance in Nineteenth-Century Poetry
(ed. with M. K. Louis)
Wordsworth and Feeling: The Poetry of an Adult Child
Sex, Life Itself, & the Original Nanaimo Bar Recipe

r a n t

G. Kim Blank

U
Umberto Press
MMII

r a n t

For further information contact
Umberto Press: Thomas Owen, General Editor
EMAIL: umbertopress@shaw.ca
Box 42086, 2200 Oak Bay Ave., Victoria,
British Columbia, Canada V8R 6T4
FAX: 250 592 6463

———————————

National Library of Canada Cataloguing in Publication Data

Blank, Kim, date
Rant

A poem.
ISBN 0-9687781-3-5

I. Title.
PS8553.L3858R36 2002   C811'.6   C2002-910410-6
PR9199.3.B49R36 2002

———————————

One section of this text ("The Heavy Weight of Snow")
appeared in the *The Susquehanna Quarterly* ©
Summer 2001. We thank Greg Fanning
for his technical creativity.

Who can distinguish darkness from the soul?
   William Butler Yeats, "A Dialogue of Self and Soul"

*In dreams the truth is learned that all good works are
done in the absence of a caress.*
   Leonard Cohen, *The Favourite Game*

These fragments I have shored against my ruins . . .
   T.S. Eliot, "The Waste Land"

r a n t

suspira de profundis
montreal, new york

The Angel of Life is the Angel of Death
And Suffering holds Bliss dear
And in Darkness so shines the Light
Through Forever runs the Now
Within Experience lives Innocence
And into Hell was Heaven taken
And in the Journey is the Quest
Within the Circle Knowledge sees
In Silence Thunder rolls
And in the End a new Start
Within all Wonder the Simple Song
And in Never sighs the Always
And in fallen Loss does Gain find wings
In Autumn's Graves live Spring's new Birth
And within Ice will Fire dance
In Beauty's Eye the Beast looks down
Through the Trickster We see God
And in Chaos Meaning and in Meaning Doubt

And so All Forms reflect their Soul
Within the Calm speaks one last Rant
One Step Forward
Two Steps Back

(ready steady go)
you might be flying
through the heavens
yet you're crawling
through a hell
no tea spoons for time
white line ticking fine
crushed into a bowl
boiled over a flame
sucked into a hose
plunged into a crease
blown into a hole

                              a shallow white grave
                                 a red grave marker
        ain't no escape no finishing tape only cornerless
                         s p a c e
             tired out tied down just out on the town
                  pulled aside shoved around
                     hanging in hanging out
                              no place for a shadow
                                 no space for a sigh

                              no room with a view
                              no time for a vision

never mind revisions
time only for crimes

                                    on the in side
                                    on the down side
                                    on the dark side

crimes down in the heart
on the bad side of town

                                where it aches
                                where you owe
                          where mysteries shun clues
                         where doors slam dead bolted
                             where windows stay shut
                              where curtains pull tight
                             where flies twitch all day

with no show for the road
with a tank stuck on empty
with no funds in the bank

                                  all cards expired
                                all deposits unsafe

withdrawals with out assets
interest charged nightly

                          there's none for the money
                           there's none for the show
                           there's none to get ready

                              there's no where to go

the light's always red
you're always yellow
the grass never green
not on your side
your side of the street

                              this tortured course
                              this hard cold way

on side walks that lick you
eyes that just flick you
in a blink
in this city this town

                              this code with out zip
                              this address of zilch
                              this rancid brick road

there's no place for a home
there's no where to roam
no mermaids to sing
no where to run
no warm rising sun
no dome decreed
no wonderland of oz

                              some where over the pain
                              some where back there

no one tips a hat
casts a line

takes your coat
makes you feel real fine
no one looks you back
nods one blessing
lends an ear
pats a back
gives one warm sign

                              before they walk on by
                              before they write you off
                              before they cross you over

stare you through
blow you off
before they suck you clean
you're dry winter dust
you spin around
look down then up
and the past slams on its brakes
the revision of a thousand nights
rises from shadows
ravens hang from posts

                              the dead awake
                              the living sleep
                              the walking dream

you spin around
look fore then back
to that first dark night

that first falling out
that forbidden tree
the serpent's smile
that first taste of death
after life's first breath
the longest day
to the flooding waters
the beasts the foul
the legion of angels
the burning lake
a stream of bodies
poured darkly from heaven
hurry to hurry fro
a torrent of gloom
through the wilderness ocean
dusty hoods shadowed motions
some flee some chase
a yoked vain race
cages ribs rattle by
bony fingers shaking die
baking birds released from pies
flying up dropping down
holding on letting go
glass eyed skulls
they gawk on by

chained to memory
noosed by history trapped by misery
pop
goes the hallowed nation
poof
goes green creation
they walk on by
pilgrims digress readers digest daughters fathers sons
bitches demons lovers witches weasels mystics
floggers gloaters floaters crooks pros pervs beauties
beasts angels lovers adams eves dreamers hopers
hangers weepers walkers keepers runners peepers
sleepers fallers ballers gunners rollers movers shak-
ers suitors crooners tutors groovers spooners takers
givers fakers masters slaves porters thinkers sorters
stinkers drivers strivers writers wrongers suckers
punters fuckers fighters hunters hucksters winners
grunters groaners losers boners boozers cruisers plan-
ners scammers stalkers squatters jurors curers sin-
ners fuhrers chicks pricks dicks coppers tellers rob-
bers buyers sellers shoppers walkers runners le.ad-
ers swappers bleeders jokers dressers smokers sow-
ers chokers growers reapers eaters brokers shysters
buyers sellers leavers dwellers phonies cronies johns
blondes nomads gonads heroes zeros stars neros pau-

pers princes twits cheaters fops wits wops jigs blacks
dikes whites saints knights jupiters lucifers dowagers
travellers fruits brutes bankers wankers spankers
wives husbands preachers flunkeys frauds teachers
bookies buddhists misfits druggists cubists sickos
psychos all walk on by

                              two
                        four sex ate
                who do you now fornicate
        one three five seven what's the odds
                  you'll go to heaven

none to slim
sink or swim
shelf the self
shun the one
count to none
its all undone
and done again
lethewards sunk still
still falling   falling
                                                   they walk on by

the human tale
the plotless trail
the weak the frail
the coffin's nail
the darkened vale

oh mother of jesus
sweet mother of all
the stumbling crawling praying
choking gagging crying
pouting wailing shouting
drums tighten fear heightens
the ins the outs
the twists the shouts
you break you drop

                                    you fall to pieces
                                    you move in side

piece

                by

                                            piece

spin your wheels
stay your place
barely stay your place
you look way up
the sky falls in

                                    they walk on by

cats grin tails twitch

                            they're on their way
                            they're lately late

every post marked date
meetings beatings rendezvous
estrangements missed arrangements

their lawyers sue

                    down that hole they all go
                 down your hole you crawl too
the one mother gave you
don't do dick
won't ever stick
will make you sick
yet you step
go your way
take the chance

                you step this way
                  you go on in
             you watch your head
hang your coat switch your face have a seat light a
smoke share a joke a laugh or two you lift a drink
nod your head

        take a breath

wait for signs

                   take it cool
                take your time
                take your time
cats grin tails twitch
have another no

                no bother at all

                                        no hurry no stall
don't mess up
settle the score
you take your time
that's all you've got
it don't take long
to sing the song
dance the dance
to borrow the look
snakes slide in side
heads pull aside
move around check you out
plexus flex sweat collects
temperature rises coolness presides
pushing providing dealing deciding
then its over
done begun again
out a side exit
up the down stairs
                                        and you're gone
falling inwards falling down
falling small turning round
the circus comes forward
your body leaves home
                        sure you had a cold coming of it
                          sure it was the dead of winter

                    sure the voices charged high prices
what of it
want a medal
want some sympathy
for some devil
                                        get a ticket
                                        get a life

wait your turn
stand in line
with all the others clutching gods
with painted idols and nunnery frauds
want some advice
listen to this (some sailor said)
slow right down (he said)
then spoke

The Centre of the Wheel
There you do not Move
You do not Live
You safely Hide
But on the Wheel's fine Edge
That turns turns turns
You Move
You fall get crushed and rise
Fall get crushed and rise once more
There you Live and do not Hide

thus spoke
(he said)
disappearing (he said)
let the parade come by
the chariots pass
the wheel rolls through
let clowns come to life
let flags raise high
let colours spread voices dance
for the moment
maybe two or three
then you'll see
then it's gone
there's something wrong
the circus packs up
the colours die clowns cry
flags fall from the sky
you run for cover
dive into a bunker
some porcelain pew
give it your guts
between a yawn and a scream

                              spilling your being
                                spilling the beans

eyes twisting back

fumbling with lies
choking on dirt licking up bile
black and white tile
on paper towel palms
you crawl through ashes
mumble more prayers
itch at vague sounds
scratch at pale letters

get it
down
run it
down

you look for the answer
claw through bleached words
stumble with phrases
stuck between chapters

your life as a typo
your worldless words
your world as a worm

under the heel
a truth turned to pulp
bad fiction turned too true
true lies turned too false
the medium needs massaging
once upon a time
no twice perhaps

                        to not be
                        or not to be
                                    there's no question
                                    there's nothing noble
sounds of silence troubled waters
through the storm
collar to the wind
heads roll ladies stroll
dice roll mouths flinch
the circle closes
these city walls
wet city walls
walks that go no where
saints marching   up
angels falling

                                    down
                        thy kingdom come
                        thy kingdom go

the condiments of sacrament
thorns oils grails smoke mirrors
the embodiments of banishment
the corpulent the consequent
the different the discontent
the fraudulent the impotent
the insolent the negligent
the penitent the punishment

the reverent the supplement
the indolent the miscontent
the beds of nails
you do not like green eggs and spam
minutes like seconds
hours like days
you've got time on your hands
could you would you
agitate calculate indicate celebrate circulate cultivate
demarcate demonstrate duplicate dominate mediate
mitigate moderate litigate lubricate penetrate
mutilate ejaculate incubate recreate separate
subjugate terminate nauseate contaminate
depopulate intimidate intoxicate
could you would you
later maybe later
nothing but time on your hands
a broken watch on your wrist
sorry thoughts on your mind
                    but you're late
                         oh
                      too late

                              out of time
                              out of step
                              out of sync
                              out of ink

with no map
with no sign

                              not a wink
                              not a nod

roads lead you follow
spoons feed you swallow
alleys like membranes
place with out person
needleless compass
needless of company
all for none
none for all

                              no true north
                              no truth no worth

all ways the same
lanes with no name
each day you give
give your self a way
each month spells
grows mounts swells
fills up spills over
runs down the side
heaps of token thoughts
floods from broken clots
frailties rain down
stolen pleas sink

the landscape shrugs
hands tied belly pulled
a crown of tin hopes

                              forks in the road
endless

                              forks in the road

your system in overload
knives for the wrist
detours like whores
whores like detours
seduced by dead ends
paths without custom
routes without numbers
tricks without treats
thoughts worth dick
ticks without tock
you pull in for a stop
a nudge and a wink
a ruby red pit
she pulls you in

                         to her holy sin
                    to her white hot skin

your body folds
she pirouettes on your bayonet
a sweaty coquette minuet
for one moment you forget

the debt and the fret and the wet
then each returns
each kiss tastes like piss
with a pull on the belt
you come away
leave behind some face
some sticky trace
some unkind embrace
a penny gets you nothing
ten thousand even less
you pay toll every step
flagged down fogged in fucked up
departing from where ever
weightless baggage weighs you down
struck off wait lists
will that be smoking or torture aisle or window cof-
fee or blood noose or injection electricity or gas white
wine or black bile fasten your seat belts you've now
entered hell
hell ya
      it all returns the broken deal the rotten stuff
            the ruby red the flightless bed
                  the rib caged race
                  the empty
                        space
the infinite night

the endless cliche
the heroless hurray

                you're a no where man
             you're in sight of blindness

time is your thief
skin your cell prison
an eternity of self
it steals from your sleep
robs every dream
time zones twilight zones
outer limits speeding tickets
no pilgrims to trust
no hands on deck
no captain to touch

               for a guide for a hint
             for a nudge or a wink
              for a pinch or a pat

they stare you move
barbies kens g i joes
they drop on by

                  the way
            every face a fugitive
        every flag waves surrender

coats without arms
bodies without heat
crusades with no purpose

                              no infidels to crush
                              no witches to burn
travel on travel on travel on babble on babylon
                   over cross walk puzzles
dictionary buildings guzzle every walking suit
                         muzzle
here a word there a word every where a word word
                              with a flick of a hand
                              with an unspoken sound
you get tossed to the side
you're riff you're raff
a never ending paragraph
you're a thousand laughs
a neckless giraffe
armed with thin foil
like meaningless toil
like chewed over gum
like spewed over rum
go ask alice

                         you're done you know it
                         you're cooked toasted boiled
neither rare nor well done
burnt in oil
burning both ends
fried until dried
you cry until dry

you're caught in

                              between

                                                        in
                              between your teeth
                                                        in
                              between the cracks

under your nails
on the roof of your mouth
a chapel of spit
pure counterfeit
phlegm for your mortar
a spittoon for a pew
a prayer for a tongue
in side your blunt head
beneath your thick skin
like a tick wiggling in

                                        between
                              fear and bad luck
                                        between
                              a blink and a beat

a rock a hard place

                                        between
                              the stars and the moon

time let you down
rubbed your face in the ground
kicked you when you were down

               made you small in side
               made you hide in side
               made you sigh cry lie

what's to deny

        so

say good bye
bounce a way

     float by like a bubble

        or

     a balloon filled with trouble
another hollow man
from a corked screwed clan
with stolen years
you were never young

          nothing ever easy
          nothing ever gold
          nothing ever green

never evergreen
but not forever
yet red white blue
one autumn morning
glistening silver blue
who could have thought
not you
two flaming arrows
from terror's desert bow

look up in the sky

                it's a bird
                it's a plane
                no it's
                it's
                it's like a movie

two flaming arrows
pearce das kapital
mirrored towers come rumbling down
people learn to fly
peter pans learn to die
a town drowns
waves of dust
women turn to salt
men turn to tears
bulls turn to bears
zeroes into heroes
you care or not
you don't need a champ
but all stare
it's like a movie
you say you said
where's willis snipes
gibson eastwood
where's hollywood when you need it
all those bodies among paper

a world wakes up
a new small smoking world
highjacked by news
making bold all you knew
makings stars out of clay
bang bang shoot shoot
but its the same old sun
the self same smoking gun
the same colour scheme
gray dull wan
pixelled swizzled swished swooshed
the same curtain call
leafless languid listless
so you find your ground
set up for the night
stumble some more
mumble some less
at last change the channel
and its back to the street
to card board castles
queens of amazombies
to voo doo arms and tattoo charms
and crying lips and whispering eyes
cold dry love
servings of sea weed
garnished with sand

king of the box cars
a ditch for a moat
draw bridge eyes
there's not much space
                    and
                                the band plays on
                              the ship sinks slowly
                                   the fog closes in

women children first
men leave next
the crew follows on
the captain waves his hat
                                   says fair thee well
                                   says fair thee well

good bye bitter dream
                                no life boat for you
                                no life left for you
                                 no life left in you
                    and
the band plays on
the ship sinks slowly
the fog closes in
drowning in shade
swimming in air
                                 the ice man cometh
                                 the ice man taketh

yet he gives you a song
says listen hold on
you've nothing to lose
so he conjures some scene
and sings of the past
he even punctuates

The branch breaks with the quiet weight of snow.
The still, brittle cold huddles all around.
Winter makes the tree, an apple, seem old,
Much older than its secret rings might tell.
Leafless, showing every knot, it stands—
Or barely stands, fruitless limbs sadly thin.
(A frail, old man in a field, as you might say,
If, on some stillborn night, you travelled through.)
At first the snow passed blindly by each branch,
But then it touched, held fast one narrow place,
Gathered slowly through the silent hours;
A growing balance so wondrously fine,
A puzzle to the eye, for those who look.
The branch held until it could bend no more.
Then it broke with the quiet weight of snow.
This tree, now carved and hardened by the cold,
Will pass the winter, and still winters more.
The leaves will come again, green through the spring,

Turn open, hopeful, to the summer sky,
And then let go come autumn's growing chill.
With no owner the fruit falls to the ground.
(He's not returned since that pale year of dust.
Some say he passes by when seasons call;
Others say he heard the ocean calling.)
Winter breaks the promise, works in silence,
Whispers to the land that an end may come.
This tree: not mine to care for, yet I watch
And wait for signs in snowy fields—of what?
The question hangs in the cold, on a single branch.
This world was never made for peace—or war,
But for narrow places and fragile limbs,
For old knotted men in still older fields,
For some journey taken without return,
For miracles of snow upon a branch.
The seasons promise little, ask no favours,
Give answers passing jays might know, who these
Quiet days are the tree's lone visitors.
So I watch the branch bend in cold silence,
A balanced moment, brief, for eye and heart,
Broken now by the quiet weight of snow.

well enough of that

                                        (he says)

enough of that indeed

italics no less
back in the day
when a poem was a poem
not an excuse just to roam
when you felt without thought
when the rope was not taught
when the urn was well wrought
          well
that was then
now is when
and here is now
so beat the drum slowly
let time do its march
let it trundle through gloom
with out space
stealing all the room
leaving no trace
it's been something
it's been nothing
a slice

                    a long time passing
                    a long time passing
          into the valley of death
          into the stone valley you go
silicone chips silicone jiggles
geeks all in giggles

hard drives soft wares
sound bites stage frights
logged out clear cut put up shut up fed up belly up
cock up mock up throw up blow up give up hold up
hold out spaced out take out fake out fall out break
out worn out stake out ball out all out all day all night
shock around the clock
chicken stock blood clots
high way by way
oathless old men
forgotten kings sit upon the ground
old bones on some old mountain
the grave diggers toil
poets trip on words
fall into holes
dig darkly the soil
headless hoarse men
tongeless trash talk
drive by shoot 'em ups
hot crossed guns bark
panicked police going gone
garbage trucks dumping running sewers running
faceless buses busing childless mothers fussing
children dragged hurried hands
empty feet no where fast
no where fast no where fast

                              so many words
                              so little sense

shoes fit like leeches
skies fade then retreat
closed down fall down get down
run down keep down in out
                              down out howl shout
                              down cast cast down
you're going down down down
down in the spine
down town rant
it's only the song
only the song
you best keep moving
don't turn around
don't turn around
icy hoods dumb prayers
embroidered brows gothic stares
death bells ring ring out
the old the new the perhaps the true
angels carved in bone
stoned angels young cold
sweet starved spirits
virgins bare foot wan
incense breath steamed sighs

all eyes vaguely gaze
looks heavy with leaden wings
foot steps echo
fevers like dew
like torn out roses
in black in white
the night's clenched fist
the day slaps your face

                              it is the same
                              it is the same

nothing going on
nothing going down
it wasn't supposed to be this way
not at all
no not at all

                         no one ever told you
                         no one said watch out

you take care you hear
one way to live
one thousand ways to die
he maketh you to lie
to lie in hardened pastures
glades of festered cement
cemeteries for secretaries
tomb stone sanctuaries
strings pulled puppets swing

ties tighten jugulars frighten
speech with out words
words words words

                              no story to tell
                              no ending to sell

no plot no scheme
no setting no theme
things fall apart
circles with out centres
words with out deeds
an unkind hush
all over the world
more than a feeling
less than a thought
looking up counting down
tin jaws thin laws
bars of sin
no next of kin
liquor is quicker
go kiss your sister
trespassers are faster
you've gone passed go

                              way past go
                              way past gone

(psst: there's a voice to hear
a voice that won't falter

the voice that's not here
it hides in the altar)
liar liar pants on fire
the voice you hear comes from the mire

                              try to call
                              do not collect

this number has changed
hang up try again
this number has changed
hang up try again
flip the quarter
tails again and again
the numbers game
wander off wonder on
you search you look
this number has changed
hang up try again
square holes round pegs
lame dancers chairless legs

                              they say you say
                              they stay you say
                              they go you stay

you wait you wait
they come they say
tomorrow never comes
today never goes

hang out hang around

                                you stay they go
                                they stay you go

try again try again

                                    it's the place
                                    it's the time

in you go
impostors pretenders offenders
all sit ugly
toads on some fence
you think but don't think
dragged through the mud pulled through the crud
cancer in a cone
a gun in your head
you join in
slide into the wall
next to the crack in the wall
real cozy and all
glass lifts your mouth
shallow swallows sink fast

                          some music some where
                              some broken chorus

a thought rings out
a fermented miscarriage

                          there's no continuum
                          there's no continuing

the thought is dropped
it's too cold for a thought
too hollow to chew on
you order another
an other another

        and then they're off
          and you're off
         and there you go

rounding first turning tight
coming from behind
coming up the rear

      no win no place no show
       no ticker tape no no

eyes turn black ashes fall
dust to dust
dusk to dusk
the loser's circle
drawn with a nail
waking dreams sleeping days
against the wall
you need to slide out
there's no way past the noise

        it's midnight at noon
        it's dark the day long

again again and again
an eclipse of the soul

                              galileo galileo

some broken chorus
what's the buzz
the window calls
the hours fall
you need the day badly
the day don't need you
                    there's no home on this range
                    there's no hope for the strange
for the ranger who's lone
                              you sit the fence
                              you walk the line

because you're nein
against the wall
the crack in us all
you think big
talk the big scene
freud's void marx's crime
eliot's pound weighs in
falls down for the count
                         some eclectic metric
                         some waste of good land
                         some modern post mortem
some litany of ginsberg tea
none for you
none for —

mind never mind never
body mind body mind
kant can descartes can't

                    no subject no object
                    no point in a sphere
                    no centre to grab
                    no sun set to sign with
                    no music to leave by
                    no laughter no encore
                    no credits no score
                    no audience roar
                    no clubs no passes
                    no special side door
                    no members to join you
                    no volume to pump

to get with the beat
you're right out of power

                    your extension extended
                    your battery not charging
                    your connections unplugged
your bulb burned out cold
rock a bye
rock a bye
a.c. d.c. d.o.a. o.d.
mary jane lucifer
knocking up heaven's door

no one home no one home
you're wired you're lost
what did you just say
how much will you pay
dead dogs in heat
smelling their own asses

                        your stinking roses
                        gun powdered noses
                        your grandma moses

mountains mole hills
needles hay stacks
snow balls hell
sermons ditches burning witches
wailing walls toilet stalls
clouds burst blades raise
two thumbs down
tune in turn on drop dead

                        some broken leary chorus
                        some window calls

the way sudden opens
the wall lets you go
the deal seals the crack
you're out but not in
will you sink
will you swim

                        the rapture of uncertainty

                                    the ecstasy of doubt
                                    the banality of finality
                                    the cheek of avante chic

oh aren't you smart
so very clever
so full of syllables
you think that plastic
is just fantastic
the pastiche of leather
so very clever
so deconstructive
you think wounds heal
but look
there's spaces filled with spaces
filled with places for spaces
unmatched forms features worn
heavy shadows lightless homes
dreamless fields sardined cabs
zoo bars unholy smoke
men at work
kids at play
one way streets
take a number
cross world puzzles
one million chameleons
your lemming friends

wham bam thank you mam
three four close the whore

                              by the sea
                              by the sea
                        by the c-u-n-t
disgrace the race abuse the muse rupture the culture
hold up your end remote with out control bugger the
tradition down with the crown up with the people
twinkle twinkle little queer
how you wonder
why you fear
toothless hags   girly mags
head lines   traffic fines
news papers scoop
vultures smiling swoop
faces lift lines fall
surgeons cut engines stall
nose jobs snow jobs odd jobs blow jobs
stories sicken plots thicken
two by two hoof by foot
forty days forty nights
drowning scenes lowered sites
mountain tops drowning valleys
over your dead body
promised land under repair
raining   raining   raining

islands in the night
lights out of reach
fading   fading   fading
imperfect lies child cries
quick sand sinking mollies
pollen headed people folly
stamens pants pealed pushers
venus zipper traps
every lasting cold
plumbers in your plexus
fasting women starving beauty
pushers in the lexus
thin maidens tin satans
they call you to the rocks
your rocking horse thoughts
the face of quiet turns a way
muzzled stilled gagged puzzled
dark spirits shady boons
heaven's brink clouded moons
sick eagles dizzy pains
dark lights big city
big deal bad deal get real
skin fold skin mold
every thing intrudes
thick as a brick
fine as a line

your tank reads e
you coast to a stop

> just then a haven
> just another craving

the address rings a bell
a pit stop in hell
a turn to the right
take a left
you sit down
order one two three
the one eyed man
that one eyed man
looks at you twice

> the music whose is it
> the rhythm the blues
> the rock the roll
> the jazz the soul
> the message comes back

its all buddha man
he's a genius man
he's the end man
it's okay man
just hang on man
ideas like smoke

in the middle

> on the edge

by the side

                                        up the creek
                    in the way
off the record
over here   over there
either nor neither or
                         how many shades of gray
                          how many words to say
                           how many bills to pay
one more for the road
just one more
four five six
and you're gone
bridges falling down
your unfair hades
stop for a light
look hey look
there's nothing in the sky
lucy's gone too high
guillotine windows cut the light
you're guilty as charged
fouls committed crimes admitted
out of order out of order
you fall down the street
open flung jerked around
pulled apart pounded

                        down
one more time
just one more time

                              it's one day past noon
                               it's too much too late
                               it's too little too soon

weeds tumble by
sands fill your eye
words fumble die
slivers run your tongue
lipless followers streaming by
a dum silent symphony

                                 you want the heart
                                  you need the beat
                                  you plead the case
                                  you want the space
                                  you lose the chase

loved like a slut
impounded like a mutt
washed out bad rinse
pounded like mince

                           like meat for the market
                            like grist for the mill
                           like targets loves bullets
                           like age loves the mirror
                            like slugs love the tear

                              like blood loves the air
                              like trees love the book
                              like fire loves smoke
                         like snakes love their bellies
straws break camels' backs
one hump or two
lambs cry in the cold
hounds lick new found wounds
wolves scream at the moon
packs gather chose their prey
lions never sleep
sheep never blink
never look behind
never close your peepers
victims peck their purses
                                        you can only watch
                                        you can only watch

pick up the scraps
the bone soup
the spare change
left over left overs
carry on carrion
you're lord of the flies
king of the crap
dead piggy no bank
the heart of a roach

bash 'em in bash 'em out
maggot faggot in slo mo
spitting out broken luck
odd queer rotten wrong
cast down cast out
slouching slutted sunk
trespassers be where

          casteless all untouchable
          no class no room no way

you're not in the ball game
you're winless all season
miracles magic nothing works
not a break to be got

          no fans in your stands
          no standing room only

you can't even stand
foul balls foul play
hitless forced out
you're caught way off base
way off base lining
sliding   sliding   sliding
          strike three you're out
          strike four strike five

swing low sweet chariot
coming for to carry you home
sunk down under heaven

a hole in the ground
no one on deck
its the bottom of the bottom
                    and

                              you need to get home
                              you need to be home
the band plays on
number nine number nine
blackened spots of time
bloated bodies stuffed with crime
faces licked with grime
cheek turned hope primed
not this time
one slap washes the other
hand outs hand in

                              you wait at the station
                              you flip through the news
oh boy oh boy
a mass disturbed nation with out masturbation crime
syndication prime indication some new sensation
new gratification star adoration bed room preoccu-
pation blocked circulation market elation globaliza-
tion third world stagnation alien infiltration broken
federation forced liberation forest preservation bible
versus creation soul and salvation a new constella-
tion bused integration worker exploitation market

fluctuation crop cultivation bug infestation fume in-
halation gene separation genetic mutation arms pro-
liferation armed invasion leaked radiation rest and
relaxation minor altercations wrong connotations
forced deportations tax evasion court mediation ef-
fect and causation burning plantation gross indigna-
tion seeking clarification more false documentation
false accusation child molestation extreme allegations
moral degradation sensory deprivation great expec-
tations final destinations final deliberation final dis-
pensation final justification final legislation white
domination clear indications new innovations bind-
ing arbitration closing liquidation close correlation
perpetuation premeditation investigations insinua-
tions less stabilization more regulations less moderni-
zation more representation less participation more
recrimination less retaliation more polarization regur-
gitation regurgitation

                              it's all the same

some wordy game
some crying shame
some worldly gain

                              all ways the same

just change the name
give the quo some status
then move along move along

you're baggage not claimed
a one way ticket
your bus left town
the gray dog ran away
a tale between its tires
scrap paper run over
your words flatten out
road kill lines

                              blown aside blown away
                              blown upwards for a ride

butts in a pot hole
litter for cats
for fish bone alleys
ash trays with sand
dust in dim corners
dirt under dull rugs
plugged drains taps drip
taps drip drip drip
sucked up on a plunger
garbage not collected
rags hardened by heat

                              wiping some street
                                wiping some ass

tenants with out land
lord you need help
words with out course

action with out source
passage with out words
a renter with out recourse
a damaged deposit
a room for the night
a bed never made
sheets never washed
sinks never rinsed
paint peeling yellow
pissed up toilets
plugged to the gills
floating fish of wet paper
pale gobs of wet paper
stained by damp guts
by the previous soul
you passed on your way
passed you the way down

who looked just like you
who smelled just like you
who might have been you

you might have been him
he relied on you
gave his life
went to war
settled a score for you
opened a door

left his wife
lied tried cried for you
said good byes
would have died for you
na na na na
hey hey hey go-od bye
clap trap crap track
day in day out
push in push out
numb dumb hum drum
roll an other
some roaches for killing
where there's smoke there's
well they all look the same
water marked ceilings
one wall two walls three walls four
mirrors in luckless pieces
puke stained floors

                    not one plate fits
                    not one cup clean
                    not one glass clear
                    not one drawer closed

broken rusted burners
piss soaked matches
chairs limp in corners

                  it will rock you to death

                              it will keep you awake
twisted lamps crippled tables
with out contents
spineless books crimeless crooks
you spread out papers
you haven't read

                                   that you couldn't read
                                   that tell you your rights
                                   that don't right the wrongs
words from the deeds
pockets in side out side in
conviction eviction prescription
discrete receipt deceit
pay your doctor
loathe thy neighbor
honour thy mother fucker
fuck you no foucault

                              your motions disguised
                              your colour soiled spoiled
                              you're eating your body
from the in side out
rancid rotted rank
an expiry date dated
the day you were born

                              your body's bagged
                              you're all left over

                                    in a doggy bag
                                you're in body bag
there's no more to come
no company for dinner
no dinner for company
                            save misery save misery
                        save memory same memory
a past passes by
a parade limps through
a history of histories
a tale too frail
so dim the lights
raise the curtain
the play's the thing
we'll hit the heights
of death we're certain
of vanity too
just let it roll
                                    and a one and a two
                                    and a one two three
oh that miltonic milton
lucky blind laconic milton
with his unsatanic satan
his infelicitous lycidas
sampson bringing down the house
walls come a'tumbling down

saint joan's tears
ahab's leg vincent's ear
cain's hard brow
actaeon's bow wow
bundy's yawn amin's taste
mengele's whims pol pot's haste
werther's sorrows kurtz's horrors
cocteaux rimbaud enfant terrible
baudelaire in under wear
beckett waiting he don't care
ghandi's feet nelson's fleet
ali's jab the yorkshire stab
plato's cave fossey's apes
nero's rome steinbeck's grapes
hannibal's alps lecter's scalps
lear's no more van winkle's snore
an ovary from bovary
moses and his burning tree
swan songs of innocence
chatterton all chatting done
byron's limp darwin's chimp
lennon's tomb plath's young womb
woolf's room norma's gloom
lowry's drunken lava dowry
jimi h janis j james d
kurt c kurt dead

sticking bullets in his head
hitler's wink stalin's smile
murder: "may I stay a while"
bombs drop children rise
targets beckon mothers cry
zeno zoro zero zappa
kubla khan kubla kant
hamlet faust voltaire proust
cohen crows dylan blows
camus kafka neitzsche nut
charlie m sharon t
helter skelter m.t.v.
jim m fires lit
paris burning open pit
suck a shot gun hemming's way
compact prose will never pay

         a happy life's not short
         a happy life don't start

short lived stories short
foot notes critic's text
names dropped who's next
brian jones no moss will gather
balushi snorting too much sushi
kennedy's mystery enemies
conspiracy smirks from every knoll
different smoke from every hole

you'll never know
the truth's out where
the truth's too false

              guns for every widow
              guns from every window
bullets hail from every glance
jackie o cups jack's blown mind
rifle sights turned crucifix
knives slit starry nights
a tackled her-o j
all rushing mounts to zero
throats bleed dogs wailing
lawyers on their bucks all sailing
end zone end game
prime time crime slime

              you see a black door
              you want to paint it —
mary's lamb blake's sheep
peter's pumpkin keats' sleep
jack's crown yeats' leap
fairy tales poets flail
pussy's well farmer's dell
dante's day in heat to dwell
high ho the merry oh
we all go to hell
rub a dub dub

three knaves in a tub
a butcher a rapist
a professional sophist

                              you put your left foot in
                              you take your left foot out
                              you swing your partner

round and round
kick her in the toilet
flush her down
where she stops
no body goes
you pull up a chair
you try to sit square   but
you're thinking you're sinking
they're floating they're gloating
you're buried deep below
(do you think they really know)
you look for harmony
find misery
you try the alphabet
instead end up on some bus
waitin' 'round waitin' 'round
yeats would be fine (you say)
if masks weren't a crime (you say)
dolls with magi
blood and the moon

milk on the stone
yes that's yeats (you say)
yeats would be fine (you say)
"the nightmare rides upon sleep"
oh that one gets you
read on read on
your life line cut short
rolled fine for a snort
a fine line in deed
to a powdered keg between your ears
there's no air left
lungs collapse wet bread

                    they sail on their knives
              they slice your scorned surface
                      butter your veins

peel through the surf
razors like rudders
fight for the turf
they cut rows of foam
they sell you one wave
served on a mirror

                  a plattered reflection
              a splattered complexion
                  a shattered direction

it won't get you to shore
it can't help any more

wiped out written off
it's the deal of a century
held over for ever
one life per customer
last chance closing down

                every thing must go
                every item marked down

cash and carry
two for one three for nothing
every detail less than retail
guaranteed in writing
proven by the reading
felt by the bleeding
that red grave marker
held down by the highest court
written in air so rare
on earth so bare
caves full of ice
it stings you to breathe
it itches to script

                all hands dealt a bad hand
                all sales final

red seas promised lands
mercury rising phoenix falling
the nazi paparazzi
humpty dumpties chicken lickens

twisted metal foot floored pedal
widow makers coffin traders
martyr makers any takers

                              the strong sell
                              the dead smell
                            the weak inherit
                         the markets bear it

praise the board
bow down to jones
common dollars uncommon sense
paper money paper backs
pages yellow scribblers hacks
pages missing over due
crippled fingers do the walk
limping mouths do the talk
preface prelude prologue stop
false start restart
no start drop

                        no date of publication
                       no way to read salvation
   the world's a word the word is out out is in in is
                         out
              up is down push is pull empty is full
                      shake it all around
brian wilson's ungrateful bed
queen bees freddy p's

no time for losers
lungs tight as night
dog breath winds howl
smokers in door ways
spitting scowl
antichrists on street corners
pan handlers crowd round
legless armless hopeless
the blind leading all the mindless
neon knee off
hopeless beyond tears
ageless beyond years
listless figures without lists
mythless discarded anchorless
shuffling   shuffling   shuffling
every step a cliff

          chicken or egg
          thought or word
          form or content
          suck or blow
          yin or yang
          flip or flop
half empty half fool
you wander lonely

               lonely as a —
               lonely as a —

well just lonely
worthless words dear willy boy
recollections on torn corduroy
you snooze you loose
it's not like you have time to choose
it's not like you're in who's who
your note a footnote
not even a scape goat
not even a quote unquote
you're lost you're lost
not found turned in
tune out turn off drop dead
tail pipes smoke stacks
pot holes drain pipes
reflections stare
dummy's froze in underwear
windows dressed to kill
prices priced as steals
glass cages steel traps
gravel towers falling up
sand castles scrape the sky
blackened mirrors housed machines
mister cleans misses screams

                        to keep you up
                      to keep you out
                to keep you off the record

                to keep you from your self
parking meters prop you up
spare change pulls you down
one memory sticks
all else slides
just one place inside
one small place left
one picture on a mental wall
one burned in image to recall
one memory won't fall

Winters then were warm
Summers cool
Nights fell without Tears
Days rose without Fear
Sheets clean as Snow
Pillows crisp like Frost
No it wasn't supposed to be this way
No one ever told You

you fight your ghosts
you box with shadows
a knock out punch
down for the count
the towel thrown in
no one in your corner

no one on your side

                                                 just a mop
                                                 just a rag
                                   just a bucket for some hag

the odds ain't too good
a lotto for not mucho
a million to none
the breakfast of losers
corn fakes porn flakes
car horns eyes scorn
a glance would be kind
the cruelest look of all

                                                 every light red
                                               every drain plugged
                                                every faucet leaks
                                                every glass cracked
                                                 every smile reeks

humming bird eyes
bottle shaped flies
what's the buzz
nothin' ever happenin'
walking down the street
do wah diddy diddy
down down the street
sliding round some feet
hiding from defeat

swallowing your fist
choking on being
end them end them
read all about them
end them end them
perchance to dream

                                        not a hope
                                  not a damn hope

night bends day breaks
chapter two never comes
to be discontinued
some other time
muffled globe shrouded world
suffer an eclipse
son of a moon
bitch of a sun
starless nights viper thoughts
the shadow of a world
the weight of a flake
the take of a fake
move on move on
rush hour rush
traffic in trafficing
embraces all rusted
down out in out
around about twist shout

shadow lands shifting sands
a drought of thoughts
a bout of fears
slap the air
kiss some ass
throw out a digit
a salute of stench

                    up to your elbows
                      up to your neck

over your head
fed up empty vacant
a house with out rooms
rooms with out doors
doors with out handles
locks with out keys
keys with out keepers
geepers weepers
where'd you get those peepers
there's too many eyes
there's too many feet

                     too little space
                     too many walls

not enough corners
there's too many falls
there's too many stairs
with out any railings

too many crosses
not enough nailings
too many boats
not enough sailings
too little success
mouths full of failings

                              too many rantings
                              too many wailings
                              too many ravings

never a saving
too little too late
time to retreat to regroup
nibble a sandwich take some soup

                              to honor defeat
                              to bunkers of boxes

sacks full of crap
bags full of rags
pockets of air
pangs voids doubts
hags for the taking
fags on the take
meat for the market
there's too many stations
not enough stops
there's too many corners

with too many cops
you're rhyming you hate it
you'll never escape it

                  you're looking for circles
                    your needing some angles
                        you're walking the line
                        you're taking the sign
              you're ain't listening real fine

you need curves
angels with wings
boards with out bends
nerves with out ends
a place in the sun

                  where it's safe to ride doubt
                   where there's never a drought

where pleasure's the principle
pain not the name
more game no gain
sudden death over time
over time time again

                and

once more once again
the light burns out
the switch flicks itself
pulls its wire

turns to you
when you can't turn on
when you just plain can't
find the light to turn on
you're burned out again
once more once again
you're a wickless candle
a doorless handle
she said so she said
a wickless candle she said again and once more
some thing like it any way

                        never ready in the dark
                        never ready for the dark

over crowds under fed
towns of dead skin
chords with no sound
blowing round blowing down
wall to wall skin
where sin cost a buck

                            a fuck for fix
                            a suck for a six

sinew for sewing
veins freshly torn
the rip of the rush
send home the dull hurt
can't bear to be born

a real crying shame
the real crying game
all the lonely people
here's where they all come from
wombs with no exit
heart shaped boxes
dark wet bags
sweetened bitter fullness
spit blood dust
hung out to dry
strung out in the breeze
clothes hangers to hang you
to dangle your unborn
blood on a coat rack
birth on a skewer

                              meant to fill clothes
                              meant to roast lambs

silent with fear
tears with out sweat
a body of thin air
what have you done
where's there to go
there's no beacon to beckon
no saviour you reckon
no sermon to mount
stops the fear dry the sweat

fills the air fills the need quiets the rush
(its only a trick) whispers beezer
(just a trick it won't stick) whispers beezer
once upon a time
one silent night
one critical mass
history split in two
the then and the now
the here and here after
the wanderer's brow
the b c the a d
the superstitious past
the fisherman's cast
based in some manger
some immaculate deception
three complete strangers
a star was stillborn
        the horn blown so far
        the price paid so high
        the word spread so wide
        the miracles so heard
belief so assured
adoration without pride
for your sins he looked up
suffering wrung out

he's carried your cross
he walked you rode
you slept he talked
he wept you mocked
you left he waited
he loved you hated
                    (love is the answer
                            he said
                    what was the question
                            he bled)
giddy up gideon
ride on through thin pages
that story of ages
gallop through pockets
light up some rockets
strike up some band
the gang's all here
or there
or somewhere   somewhere
o sweet jesus
swinging low from on high
preaching pie in the sky
you just want some hero
                        some body to fall to
                        some trinity or other

                                    some godhead to bother
                                    some pillar to bleed on
one cup full to feed on
you turn over rocks
look for light through the night
instead find dead weight
                                    some one to stone with
                                      some one to cream on
                                    some one to score from
                                        some one too far
                                        too far to be held
naught's left but the night
grab it tight
don't let go
screw michaelangelo
the crowd that crowds in
hides from the cold
grows cracked lips
lifts meatless stews to toothless mouths
unsmooth skin unwashed hands
sockless shoes footless walks
headless thoughts soulless hopes
the weight of the world
the crushing mass
pushes from behind
falls on your shoulders

hangs on your lids
pulls on your guts
tugs on your heart
squeezes your sore spot
grabs at your balls
won't let them go
turns them twists them

                like dough for the oven
                like buns for baking

let it be let it be

            no women here come and go
            no women would come near
                no women speak

not even in tongues
tasteless sound sightless smell
one moment sticks
all else slides
all else slides
oh to be tucked in
once more pillows fluffed
nighty knighted blankets spread
a bedtime story gently read
where children dance recklessly
sing and prance happily
where valleys shine golden egged
where rainbows end

where pots of gold
where chests of jewels
blessed by a princess
where big bad every things
where ugly old who evers
get chopped up burned up
eaten up leave the valley
where kinder gentler folk live free
and tyranny flees to the hills
where ding dong witches die
where beast and beauty see eye to eye
where cyclops giants fall from the sky
where roads paved with gold
where dragons kneel
where goodness wins

                        all is well again
                 all live happily after ever

after all after all
happily ever after
the book is closed
the lights click off
nighty knighted blankets spread

                    well it just ain't so
                       it just ain't so

happily never lasting
not here not now

down town rant
you've waged your soul
bet your bottom dollar
watched the lilies sink
the rose turn to dust
flesh becomes rank
here the snow queen collects
charges by the ounce
snow white lives in a hole

                                    in your pocket
                                        in your face

mirror mirror on the table
who's the deadest in this fable
the beast eats beauty
the troll gets the goats
the witch cooks the little children
the dragon kills the prince
the giants eats the folks
wander not far from home
mother father this is not
not at all camp granada
fly a way little boy blue
pop crackle snap
ding dang dong
sheeps' blood bull's balls
dove soup pigeon stools

fools on hills mules on pills
speed kills cheap thrills
out cast scorned out
settle down take a breath
get in line
don't jump the cue
next please keep in line
who do you know
no barging in
those two those two

                              no not you not you

don't jump the cue
freud slips in again
(that's twice now
but who's counting)
jung dreaming sips on gin
skinner boxed by so thin
alice dreaming passes by
exit ophelia grave yard bound
pale trembling out of time
no more no more
breeding sin slipping in
the hall is full the show is done
time to go so simple slow time to go
the line dissolves
skies gray side walks

clouds like sighs
it rains down spit
pains in your chest
down down behind your chest
behind filth behind shame
your garbage can ribs
trash can wells despair
feasts for living dead
sucking up the waste

> from the rotting cores
> from the chewed over fat
> from the licked over bones
> from the wordless sorrow
> from your useless strife
> from your lifeless life

yes your life your life
ain't worth spit
ain't worth shit
all roads being
a detour to the ditch
all sights seeing
a view from the scab
a body that holds you
a head full of lead
hands needing bread
that won't let go

                                        that red grave marker
                                        that hole to the in side
through teeth rough as roads
through eyes thick as marble
down your throat like a gutter
sewer veins water mains
flow to the oceans
wash up on shores
a message in a bottle
forget forgive forever
                                        all things rule the heart
                                        all things rack the mind
through all temptation
through all negation
all things rule the heart
                                                far from home
                                                far from home
broken glass tin can bath
split ends on your skull
stuck in your head
                                            like shit to a boot
                                            like gum to a bench
                                            like flesh to a leech
the bus stops
the fuck stops here
doors swing open

the long ride ends

> the end of the line
> the short stick end
> the short white line

it's hope it's fear
twin destinies
swallowed tongues sing out
the choir holds its breath
swollen feet step out
tears never land
never never land
looks float across the sky
heads fall from vice
dry throats tightened necks
head heart head heart
hollow guts sore palms
red eyes black nails
christ on the cross
not forgiving you
(he's nothing terrible
it's just a parable)

> no army for salvation
> no cross to be carried

a crucial fiction where

> no one's to blame
> no one forgives

                              no body came
                              no body came

what's that you say
and you say
once again you say
say what what's that
speak up bring it up
would you do it again
the same way again
no not on your life
not with your wife
no you do not like
green eggs or ham
find the word
just one word
time is at hand
winter comes too soon
spring took a hike
the season's revelation
alpha omega naught in between
tocks ticks clocks peal
the end is near
the pages clear

                              the last dance
                              the final chord

trumpet voices seven seals

seven churches seven hills
seven sins seven stones
seven golden candle sticks
sounds of waters
second comings final judgements
light and salvation
the breath of gentle cruelty
the green green pastures
the valley of the shadow
the cup running over

                            seven stars seven ghosts
                              seven horns seven eyes
                              seven plagues one host

four angels four beasts
seven heads ten horns
four corners four winds
stars fall moons bleed
mountains burn seeds rot
bloody prophets bloodless deeds
twelve pearls twelve gates
one word rhymes with see
the other puns with eye
catch — drop —
hold — fold —
raise — up
centers once more can not hold

diamonds break waves flatten
birds fall mountains shake
send — some where
send — some where
there's no time after time
day after day
lead — not
lead — not
then you and —
make the slow way home
weave through the valleys
stagger up the alleys
wait for the visit
listen for the wind
for the knock on the door
no chinny chin chin
the devil calls
the hoofed redeemer
the wolf in sheep's clothing
the devil is dirty
he don't play clean
he's in side he's mean
he hurts o christ
thorns oils grails
hollow be thy name

nein is the kingdom
can you say it now
can you say it now
keep the words
for they are written
finally at last
one last plea
let's go and see
will the words appear
will the wind die down
will the forest hush
the desert cool
will the night fall gentley
the sun rise full
still
just

one	more	time
one	last	breath
one	more	rhyme
one	last	crime

(ready steady go)

let me out
let me in
let me sink
let me swim

                                        let me go
                                        let me stay

keep me clean
lick my wounds
clear my skin
wash my hands
heal my feet
let me breathe
move my tongue
raise my eyes
rinse my soul
scrub my wings

                                        let me fly
                                        let me rise
                    let me enter the kingdom that comes
that floats in the skies
far above where
where it hurts
from down here
where it hurts

                                 the sun burns out
                                 the sky looks down
                                 the earth opens up
                                 the sea closes 'round

the water of life
the quiet weight of snow

the edge of the wheel
the fruit of the tree
ever lasting warm
a history of history
one final flash
one rose petal
one clear pond
a feather dancing in the wind
one globe of wax
one
    fallen
       glance

Sleep my Wonder
Sleep Tonight
Don't worry any More
The Wind will soon die down
Waves will break upon the Shore
That dark pained Voice will wash away
As you sink into the Night
Your Breath will float as Music
Hold on until the Light
Hold on until the Light

~end~

r a n t
Text set in Palantino 11 point
Printed on 70 lb Fusion Opaque Cream
Acid-free, 50% recycled
October 2002
Cover design by Umberto Press

G. Kim Blank writes from Vancouver Island, where he was born.
He has lived in Vancouver, Calgary, Montreal, New York,
Southampton, Wales, and Namibia.
He presently lives in Victoria, British Columbia,
and works at the University of Victoria.